Experiencing the Good Shepherd:
Finding Rest for your Weary Soul

This page is intentionally left blank.

Experiencing the Good Shepherd:
Finding Rest for your Weary Soul

Synithia L. Williams

Copyright © 2025 by Synithia L. Williams

All rights reserved. No part of this publication may be reproduced, distributed, or transmitted in any form or by any means, including photocopying, recording, or other electronic or mechanical methods, without the prior written permission of author and/or publisher, except in the case of brief quotations embodied in critical reviews and certain other noncommercial uses permitted by copyright law.

For permissions requests, contact:
Kabillionaire Academy
Steger, Illinois
info@kabillionaire.com
708-414-6183

Book design by ParminderK

Published by Kabillionaire Academy
Steger, Illinois
https://www.kabillionaire.com/

Printed in the United States

First Edition: January, 2025

This book is dedicated to my beloved family—Marcellus, Jamela, Marcellus Jr., Micah, and Matthias.

Thank you for your unwavering love, support, and the time and space you've given me to complete this journey. I love you all deeply!

Acknowledgements

First, I want to honor my Heavenly Father for blessing me with the gifts I've been entrusted with. I am forever grateful that You have chosen me for this purpose in Your kingdom.

I also want to acknowledge my late father, Apostle James Dorsey. Thank you for raising me in the way I should go, for recognizing and nurturing the gifts within me. Your love and wisdom continue to shape who I am today.

To my mother, Pastor Cynthia Dorsey: Thank you for your unending love, your guidance, and for always pushing me toward greatness. I love you more than words can express.

To my spiritual covering, Apostle Greg and Pastor Tina Jacobs: Thank you both for believing in me and lifting me up during one of the toughest transitions of my life. Apostle Jacobs, your constant encouragement has propelled me toward greatness. I am so grateful. I love you both.

To my armor bearer, Sheila Primas: Your unwavering support, constant presence, and outpouring of love have been a source of strength. Through your mentoring, I've found my confidence. Thank you from the depths of my heart. I love you deeply.

To my sisters, Apostle Selena Williams Randall and Jaquiya Dorsey, my niece Lakirah Pegues, Uncle Gene and Aunt Fredreka Dorsey: You have been my fiercest cheerleaders. Thank you for your endless encouragement. Your love keeps me going. I love you all dearly.

Last but never least, to my church family at Harvest of Souls Ministries Intl: You all are truly amazing! Thank you for your love, support, and faithfulness.

This page is intentionally left blank.

Contents

	Introduction	1
Chapter 1	Our Shepherd	3
Chapter 2	I Shall Not Want	9
Chapter 3	Resting and Restoring	14
Chapter 4	The Valley of the Shadow of Death	21
Chapter 5	The Rod of Comfort	26
Chapter 6	The Prepared Table	30
Chapter 7	Anointed with Oil	34
Chapter 8	Dwell	38
	Summary	42
	References	43

This page is intentionally left blank.

Introduction

The 23rd Psalm is one of the most beloved and timeless passages of Scripture. In its simplicity and depth, it offers timeless wisdom about the unchanging character of God as our Shepherd. A Good Shepherd who lovingly guides, protects, provides, and comforts His sheep. Through its verses, we find the reassurance of God's divine care and His intimate involvement in every detail of our lives. God's love meets our deepest needs, restores our souls, and leads us to a place of eternal rest and peace. This book is an invitation to walk through Psalm 23 verse by verse, exhibiting the profound truths and personal applications it offers.

In these chapters, we will explore the many facets of the Good Shepherd's relationship with us. We will see Him as the Provider who meets every need, the Protector who shields us from harm, and the Comforter who brings peace even in the darkest valleys. We will reflect on His rod and staff, which bring both correction and guidance, and we will marvel at His prepared table, anointed oil, and promise of dwelling in His presence forever.

This book is not just about understanding Psalm 23 with our minds but about letting its truths settle deep into our hearts. Each chapter is designed to encourage you to reflect on your relationship with the Shepherd and to remind you that you are never alone. Whether you are walking through green pastures or the valley of the shadow of death, He is with you—leading, restoring, and covering you with His love.

As you read, take time to meditate on the Scriptures, engage with the reflections, and listen for the Shepherd's voice. Let this book be a tool to draw you closer to Him, to help you rest in His care, and to trust in His faithfulness no matter what life brings.

So, let's begin this journey together, knowing that the Shepherd is walking beside us every step of the way.

1 OUR SHEPHERD

Psalm 23:1 *"The Lord is my shepherd ……"*

Notice how the writer makes a statement of ownership as it relates to his relationship with Jesus: The Lord is MY shepherd. He makes it personal. His gives a clear viewpoint of the Lord's role in his life and his role in their relationship.

In any relationship, it is very important that roles are identified and assigned. Therefore, when roles are clearly established you know what to expect and how to respond.

The Lord is MY Shepherd! What is a shepherd?

A shepherd is someone who tends to sheep. The word "tend to" means to take care of, look after, direct, manage, nurture, cultivate and to wait on as a servant. A Shepherd is a protector, Guide, and Provider. A shepherd ensure the health of the sheep, and shear the sheep which means he cuts their wool when necessary to promote growth.

Look at the role of a shepherd. A shepherd is an authoritative figure who takes sole responsibility of caring for his sheep. A shepherd's job is not only to provide for his sheep, but to make sure they are developing and growing as they are supposed to.

When we look at the role of the shepherd, it's just not a supportive role but more of a lead role. Which means you completely put your life and well-being into the hands of the shepherd. That will be easy if you don't have trust issues and/or control issues. *Selah!*

So, the question is: Have you truly made the Lord your Shepherd?

To truly answer that, you have to understand what a sheep is.

According to Definitions from Oxford Languages, a sheep is:

1. A domesticated ruminant animal with a thick woolly coat and (typically only in the male) curving horns. It is kept in flocks for its wool or meat, and is proverbial for its tendency to follow others in the flock.
2. A person who is too easily influenced or led.

Sheep are created by God, they are timid, defenseless creatures, which are easily influenced or led. They cannot defend themselves because they do not possess any fighting skills. They are the only animals on earth like that. They are followers not leaders, they are completely dependent on someone to lead them. So, they are considered to be dumb and directionless.

A Real-Life Example:

In 2005, in ISTANBUL, Turkey, one sheep jumped off a cliff to its death, and about 1,500 more sheep followed. Of these, 450 sheep were pronounced dead. How did this happen? Where were the shepherds? The shepherds left the sheep to graze while they went to have breakfast (CBS News). Because the shepherds were not nearby, the sheep followed another sheep (may have been an older sheep) not realizing they were being led to danger. This has happened other times as well, many would probably say it was because of the neglect of the shepherds.

Sheep are highly social creatures. They band together during grazing so they follow each other. I'm sure the shepherds never thought the sheep would jump off the cliff, they probably thought the sheep were safe because they were grazing and the shepherds were close enough to see it happen, but not close enough to redirect them.

Similarly, whenever we feel the Shepherd (the Lord) is away or is not near to us where we can feel Him, sense Him, or even hear Him—we look for other things or people to fill what seems to be a void. And we will find ourselves like these sheep, falling prey to our own demise.

After looking at the definition of a sheep, many of us might resist identifying as sheep: *"I'm not a sheep, dumb and directionless!"* However, the truth is—we are. That's why we need a Shepherd. It's not until we realize we are sheep that we can't truly allow the Lord to be our Shepherd.

Wow! Chew on that for a moment.

Sheep are described as:

- Meek
- Usually very quiet
- Gentle
- Tend to listen to their leaders and show esteem to them
- Able to recognize their shepherd's voice and follow it when they hear it (and not other shepherds)
- Unable to get up on their own if they fall—they need someone to help them get up
- Picky eaters
- Continuously producing wool—the more it is sheared, the more it produces.

Psalm 100:3 AMP

Know and fully recognize with gratitude that the LORD Himself is God; it is He who has made us, not we ourselves [and we are His]. We are His people and the sheep of His pasture.

Reflection

Take a moment to reflect on the Lord being your Shepherd. Get to a quiet place. Close your eyes. Play soft worship instrumentals (optional).

_____
_____
_____
_____
_____
_____
_____
_____

Deep Breathing- Take a deep breath to the count of 4, hold it for 6 seconds, release it to the count of 7 (repeat 3 times).

_____
_____
_____
_____
_____
_____

Reflection

Meditate on Psalm 23:1- *"The Lord is my shepherd; I shall not want."*

(5 minutes)

Write what you heard during your time of meditation.

_____

_____

_____

_____

_____

_____

_____

_____

_____

_____

_____

_____

_____

_____

_____

_____

2   I Shall Not Want

This is a very strong, definitive statement.

Want (chācer - Hebrew): to lack, to be lacking, to be without, to have a need, to decrease, or to fail.

One of the hardest things in this faith walk is being in the need of basic essential things and having faith that everything will work out. When I say *basic essentials,* I mean things like food, money to pay bills, clothes, just things you need for daily living. I used to stress a lot about how things would work out. My husband's approach was just to have faith and believe, Saying, "Don't stress about it." To me, his approach was dismissive and was not getting anything done. I'm someone who never likes to ask anyone for anything. I believe everyone has their own problems and don't want to add mine to their plate. Moreover, I struggle with asking for help because I fear rejection. So, I learned over the years how to stop stressing and instead going to my Heavenly Father with my requests. **James 4:2** reminds us: *"You do not have because you do not ask God" (NIV).* As I began getting the revelation of that scripture, along with **Psalm 23:1** *"The Lord Is my shepherd, I Shall Not Want"*, I realized that any lack I was facing in my life was because I had not put it in the hands and trust my Shepherd who is responsible to make provision for me.

Wow! Literally, all I have to do is ask Him and if it's according to His will for my life, He will provide. Now I will be honest, it took some time for me to learn how to walk in this revelation. It's more than just asking, but it's asking in faith.

1 John 5:14 AMP

This is the [remarkable degree of] confidence which we [as believers are entitled to] have before Him: that if we ask anything according to His will, [that is, consistent with His plan and purpose] He hears us.

We must believe that Abba is near and that He hears us when we call on Him and pray to Him for what we need. He will make provision for us. As the Good Shepherd, He provides everything that we need. There are times we don't have to ask Him, because he knows what we stand in need of before we even ask Him.

Matthew 6:8 AMP

So do not be like them [praying as they do]; for your Father knows what you need before you ask Him.

I have experienced this personally. People have sent me money not knowing what I needed at the time, but because the Lord impressed upon their hearts to send it and they did. There have been times when I did not have food in my house, and someone rang my doorbell and said, "The Lord told me to give this to you." And, it was money to go and buy groceries. People have offered to buy me food for my home, clothes for me and my children, even pay off bills and so on—simply because the Lord, my Shepherd knew my needs and met them.

Whew! How wonderful is our God. It's such a blessing to know He hears us and loves us so much that He will provide for us. Thank you, Jesus!!!

So, I now rest in the assurance that what I can't do for myself, God can and will do. I trust that He will not leave me in a state of lack. Because with Him, I Shall Not Want.

REFLECTION

Take a moment to reflect on areas in your life where you have experienced lack. Now meditate on the part of the scripture that says: *"I SHALL NOT WANT"*. Get to a quiet place. Close your eyes. Play soft worship instrumentals (optional).

_____
_____
_____
_____
_____
_____
_____

Deep Breathing- Take a deep breath to the count of 4, hold it for 6 seconds, release it to the count of 7 (repeat 3 times).

_____
_____
_____
_____
_____
_____

Reflection

Meditate on Psalm 23:1b– *"The Lord is my shepherd; I shall not want."* (5 minutes)

Write what you heard during your time of meditation.

_____
_____
_____
_____
_____
_____
_____
_____
_____
_____
_____
_____
_____
_____
_____
_____

3 Resting and Restoring

Psalm 23:2-3 KJV

He maketh me to lie down in green pastures: he leadeth me beside the still waters. [3] He restoreth my soul: he leadeth me in the paths of righteousness for his name's sake.

One of the most important things in life that gives us strength and the ability to continue to go on in life is rest. Rest rejuvenates us, restores us, and refreshes us.

One of the definitions of rest, according to Merriam-Webster dictionary, is "peace of mind or spirit."

Ponder on that for a moment:
When was the last time you experienced peace of mind?

In ancient times, the Shepherd had to go search for green pastures. Sheep can only lie down in green pastures when they feel comfortable and safe, knowing they are provided for. At that moment, they have no care in the world.

Green symbolizes health, nourishment, growth, harmony, freshness, and fertility. Green has strong emotional correspondence with safety. It is also associated with money, which represents provision.

Sheep only drink from calm waters, and the Shepherd would go ahead of them to find waters that was calm. Restful waters signify a place of rest, trust, and confidence.

In order to rest, we need peace. **Phillipians 4:7** reassures us that it is the peace of God that will guard our heart and minds in Christ Jesus. The father gives us a peace that is unexplainable and surpasses all understanding. When I should be losing my mind, there is a calmness, an inner peace that is keeping me.

THANK YOU, LORD, FOR MAKING ME TO LIE DOWN IN GREEN PASTURES….

Of course, there is a pre-requisite to receiving that peace. Verse 6 of Phillipians 4 tells us not to be anxious or worried about anything. Now, I know you may be saying, "That is easier said than done. How is it possible to not worry or fret about anything?" Well, the verse continues to say: *"In everything, every circumstance and situation, make your specific request known by prayer and petition."* Basically, give it to the father and allow him to be the Good Shepherd that He is and provide what you need. Your only job is to rest.

Philippians 4:6-7 AMP

Do not be anxious or worried about anything, but in everything [every circumstance and situation] by prayer and petition with thanksgiving, continue to make your [specific] requests known to God. [7] And the peace of God [that peace which reassures the heart, that peace] which transcends all understanding, [that peace which] stands guard over your hearts and your minds in Christ Jesus [is yours].

When you rest, He will restore your soul.

THANK YOU, JESUS!!!!!

To restore means to repair or renovate something so it can return to its original condition or purpose (Oxford Languages Dictionary).

During a storm, what most Sheep do is stand right in the midst of the field, huddled together. Even though they have shelter, they still will stand in the midst of the field. Eventually, once they get tired and worn out from standing after the storm, they will just lay in the field. One shepherd says when he sees his sheep laying out there, he just gently walked amongst them—not to disturb them, but to give them comfort in their state of weariness, bringing them rest.

Sometimes, during hard times, we need companions to help us stand so that we won't buckle under the pressure of the storm, giving us a sense of security and letting us know we are not alone. **Psalm 34:7** lets us know we are encamped around with the angels of the Lord. We are not alone—they help us fight.

Psalm 34:7 AMP

The angel of the LORD encamps around those who fear Him [with awe-inspired reverence and worship Him with obedience], And He rescues [each of] them.

After the storm is over, now you can lay in the green pastures and rest.

The Father doesn't only want to give us rest, but meaningful rest. That while we rest in Him, He restores every part of our soul that has been wounded, torn, broken, and worn during the storms of life.

Even if I go astray, He won't let me go too far without bringing me back, Health, finances, family heartache, grief, whatever it is, He restores me. He brings me back to the proper place. Why, you ask? Because He leads me down the path of righteousness. As long as I keep my focus on the Shepherd, He will lead me in the right direction. If I get off course, no worries —He will come find me and put me right back on the right track. I'm so glad to know He doesn't leave me out there but make sure I am headed in the right direction for my life.

I couldn't ask for anyone greater than the Good Shepherd.

Reflection

Pray This Prayer

Father, I thank you for giving me rest. Even when the road seems uneasy and so much is going on around me, I thank you that I will find peace in you. Help me to trust you with all my cares. And as I rest, thank You for restoring me.

In Jesus' name, I pray, Amen!

Write your thoughts here.

_____
_____
_____
_____
_____
_____
_____
_____
_____

Reflection

4 The Valley of the Shadow of Death

Psalm 23:4 AMP

Even though I walk through the [sunless] valley of the shadow of death, I fear no evil, for You are with me; Your rod [to protect] and Your staff [to guide], they comfort and console me.

Oftentimes in this life, we find our journey leads us into very dark times. During these times, it's hard to navigate through the fear of the darkness we are experiencing. Darkness can mean a lack of light, or a gloomy or depressed time, or a lack of knowledge or enlightenment. Darkness also can be defined as evil or wicked.

Take a moment to think about times where it seemed dark in your life, you could not see the light or anything good happening. You felt like there was no way out and no way for you to recover. Darkness impairs your vision. *You can't see at all, so how do you find your way out?*

Sheep does not like dark places. But there are times when the sheep, while being led by the shepherd, must go through dark places. Along our journey with the Shepherd, we will also have to go through darkness.

But there is no need to fear—the Shepherd is here! Smile and give God praise!!!

The valley of the shadow of death is a deep, dark place. As night sets in, the valley becomes even darker, and now the sheep cannot see anything. They begin to feel fear and anxiety, but it's in those places that the shepherd can lead by his voice alone. And the sheep would find comfort and direction in the shepherd's voice.

In order for a shepherd to lead his sheep, the sheep must first learn to know and trust the shepherd's voice.

Sheep learn the voice of the Shepherd by consistently hearing it. When a new sheep comes into the hands of a new shepherd, it doesn't recognize his voice. But sheep are good at banding together with the other sheep. And they will follow each other. Therefore, when the shepherd calls and the sheep that knows that shepherd's voice run to him, the new sheep will follow them and do the same.

Even though the sheep is not sure rather or not it can trust this voice, it will stand back and watch what he does with the other sheep. It keeps its distance until it realizes, *I can trust him.* A good shepherd is patient with the sheep. In order to train the sheep's ear to his voice, he keeps calling them.

Once a sheep learns to trust his shepherd's voice, he will be willing to follow him, even when times get difficult and it can't see the way.

The sheep eventually reach a point where there is no fear because the Good Shepherd is with them. He will never leave them alone, even if he has to sacrifice his life. He remains there with them.

The Shepherd is always with us, in every moment, including the darkest ones. And He is there to lead us through those moments back to the light. Trust the Shepherd to lead you through the valley of the shadow of death.

Reflection

When in the valley of the shadow of death, how have you allowed the Shepherd to lead you through it?

_____
_____
_____
_____
_____
_____
_____
_____

Is it easy or hard for you to recognize the Shepherd's voice?

_____
_____
_____
_____
_____
_____
_____
_____

Reflection

Do you trust the Shepherd to lead you through your toughest times?

_____
_____
_____
_____
_____
_____
_____
_____
_____
_____
_____
_____
_____
_____
_____
_____
_____

5 THE ROD OF COMFORT

Psalm 23:4b AMP

……. Your rod [to protect] and Your staff [to guide], they comfort and console me.

A rod is a natural symbol of authority and the tool used by a shepherd to correct and guide his flock.

The Shepherd's rod is used for different reasons:
1. For the protection of the sheep from the enemies.
2. For the correction or discipline of the sheep.

The staff is symbolic of leadership and authority. The staff has a curved hook at the end; therefore, if a lamb wanders or strays, the shepherd uses the hook's end to catch the lamb and bring it back. It is used to lead and manage the sheep.

He uses it to keep His sheep close to Him.

How do I find rest in comfort in the Shepherd's rod? By understanding that there are times we, as sheep, find ourselves getting lost. Lost in our ways, lost in life, lost in what to do, lost in what to believe, lost in doubt, lost in fear—just lost. But because the Shepherd is so good, He won't allow us to remain lost.

Matthew 18:12-14 AMP speaks of this:

"What do you think? If a man has a hundred sheep, and one of them gets lost, will he not leave the ninety-nine on the mountain and go in search of the one that is lost? [13] And if it turns out that he finds it, I assure you and most solemnly say to you, he rejoices over it more than over the ninety-nine that did not get lost. [14] So it is not the will of your Father who is in heaven that one of these little ones be lost."

This passage lets us know that the Shepherd is willing to leave all the other sheep to find the one that is lost. He will not stop searching for him until he is found and rejoices over it once it is found.

Rest assured, the Shepherd will not allow you to get too far away from Him before reeling you back into His ark of safety.

Reflection

Have there ever been a time you felt lost?

_____
_____
_____
_____
_____
_____
_____
_____

What did the Shepherd do to bring you back to your rightful place in Him?

_____
_____
_____
_____
_____
_____
_____
_____

Reflection

6 THE PREPARED TABLE

Psalm 23:5 AMP

You prepare a table before me in the presence of my enemies. You have anointed and refreshed my head with oil; My cup overflows.

There is nothing like having a good meal and having someone to prepare it for you. As I read over this verse, I can imagine the Father bringing me in front of a table that is full of all sorts of food prepared just for me. While my enemies lie in wait, hoping for my demise, the Shepherd has set a perimeter of protection around me. All they can do is watch me eat in frustration. He has truly prepared a table for me in the presence of my enemies.

As we research shepherds, we see that when shepherds prepare grazing areas for their sheep, they go into the fields to cut grass and pluck up weeds, ensuring it is good for the sheep to eat. Shepherds also search for patches of grass for their sheep to feast on. However, in these same areas, vipers often burrow holes in the ground for shade. Anything that walks above these holes risks being lunged at and attacked. To prevent this, shepherds would pour olive oil into the holes to make them slippery, making it impossible for the vipers to lunge forward.

As the shepherd prepares the field for the sheep to graze, they also make sure there is no potential threat lying in wait to harm them. At the first sign of a threat, the shepherd neutralizes it.

The Good Shepherd goes before us to prepare the way. **Deuteronomy 31:8 NIV** says: *"The LORD himself goes before you and will be with you; he will never leave you nor forsake you. Do not be afraid; do not be discouraged."* We do not have to be afraid because the Shepherd will make every crooked path straight, enabling us to succeed in the presence of our enemies.

Reflection

Take time to thank the Shepherd for your success in life!

Reflection

7   Anointed with Oil

Psalm 23:5 AMP

You prepare a table before me in the presence of my enemies. You have anointed and refreshed my head with oil; My cup overflows.

During the warmer months, flies swarm around the sheep to annoy them. They often land on the sheep to lay eggs, which can get into their eyes, ears, and nose, driving the sheep insane. This irritation causes them to hit their heads against trees and rocks in an attempt to rid themselves of the annoyance. To prevent this, the shepherd would take oil and rub it all over the sheep—on their heads, ears, eyes, nose, and down their back. This oil kills the flies and larvae and repels others, keeping the sheep calm and preventing them from harming themselves.

Psalm 23:5 says, *"You have anointed and refreshed my head with oil."* The oil represents the Holy Spirit. The Holy Spirit's role is to protect and deliver us from evil. **John 14:26** teaches us that the Holy spirit is our helper. **Matthew 6:13** includes the prayer to not be led into temptation but to be delivered from all evil.

The Holy Spirit is with us to help lead us in the right direction and to shield us from all evil. Just as the shepherd applies oil to the sheep's eyes, ears, and nose to prevent enemy penetration, so is the Holy Spirit that is poured out upon and within us to protect us from the works of the evil one. The more we allow the Holy Spirit to work within us, the more we become 'oily' or 'slippery' to the enemy. Our ear gates, eye gates and nose are guarded, ensuring that the plans of the enemy cannot succeed against us.

Thank God for His protection. Without it, we would be just like the sheep—running around, hitting our heads on everything, and driving ourselves insane.

Reflection

Take a moment to reflect on all the times and ways the Lord has protected you. Get to a quiet place. Close your eyes. Play soft worship instrumentals (optional).

_____
_____
_____
_____
_____
_____
_____

Deep Breathing- Take a deep breath to the count of 4, hold it for 6 seconds, release it to the count of 7 (repeat 3 times).

_____
_____
_____
_____
_____

Reflection

Meditate: *"He anoints my head with oil."* (5 minutes)

Write what you heard during your time of meditation. Also what did you feel?

_____

_____

_____

_____

_____

_____

_____

_____

_____

_____

_____

_____

_____

_____

_____

_____

_____

8 DWELL

Psalm 23:6 AMP

Surely goodness and mercy and unfailing love shall follow me all the days of my life, And I shall dwell forever [throughout all my days] in the house and in the presence of the LORD.

Notice To Dwell means to remain or live for a time. As long as we remain in the presence of the Lord, we are secure. We are promised safety in **Psalm 91:1:** *"He who dwells in the secret place of the Most High shall abide under the shadow of the Almighty."* He covers us and keeps us safe. We find rest when we feel safe and secure. Jesus, the Good Shepherd, covers us as long as we remain with Him. Temptation will try to draw us away from the Lord, but if we want to stay in the ark of safety, we must dwell in the house of the Lord. Life is so much better in the ark of safety.

In ancient times, the shepherd would sleep right at the entry of the gate, guarding the sheep day and night to make sure no one could come in or go out without his knowing.

When it was time for the sheep to go out, the shepherd would lead them. Because they recognized his sound and voice, they would move at his command.

Jesus is the same way with us. In **John 10:9,** Jesus says: *"I am the door. If anyone enters by Me, he will be saved, and will go in and out and find pasture."* He is the door, and as long as we are in Him, the enemy cannot destroy us. Amen!!!

Reflection

Will you dwell in the house of the Lord forever like David?

_____

_____

_____

_____

_____

_____

_____

_____

Ask the Lord to help you remain in Him.

_____

_____

_____

_____

_____

_____

_____

Reflection

Summary

The 23rd Psalm is more than just words on a page—it is a heartfelt depiction of the Shepherd's deep love and care for His sheep. Each chapter highlights a unique aspect of God's provision, protection, and presence in our lives. From the gentle leading to still waters to the assurance of His rod and staff, we are reminded of His constant attention and loving guidance. The Shepherd's prepared table demonstrates His abundant blessings even in the face of challenges, while the anointing with oil assures us of His healing and protection. The promise of dwelling in His house forever speaks of the peace and security that come from remaining in His presence.

This book is not just an exploration of Psalm 23; it is an invitation to experience its truths personally. The Shepherd is not distant; He is near—leading, comforting, and blessing us at every step of life's journey. As you carry these reflections with you, may you be encouraged to trust in His unfailing love, walk confidently in His care, and rest in the assurance that goodness and mercy will follow you all the days of your life. Take these words to heart, knowing the Shepherd is always with you, faithfully guiding you home.

References

1. Tecarta Bible Amplified Version
   tecartabible.com

2. Merriam Webster Dictionary
   [Merriam-Webster: America's Most Trusted Dictionary](#)

Image Courtesy: Gordon Jonson, ArtRose, Jeff Jacobs, Clker-Free-Vector-Images and openClipart-Vectors from Pixabay

Notes

Notes

Notes

Notes

Made in the USA
Monee, IL
12 February 2025